D1495364

The Mystery of Faith

Father Tadeusz Dajczer

The Mystery of Faith

Meditations on the Eucharist

PARACLETE PRESS
BREWSTER, MASSACHUSETTS

The Mystery of Faith: Meditations on the Eucharist

2009 First Printing

Copyright © 2009 by Bolesław Szewc

ISBN 978-1-55725-686-7

Original title: *Tajemnica wiary*
Translated by Artur Polit, preedited by Rev. Bryan Storey with edits for this
Paraclete Press edition, first published in October 2009.

Imprimatur
  +George W. Coleman, D.D., S.T.L.
  Bishop of Fall River, Massachusetts
  October 22, 2009

  The imprimatur *is an official declaration that a book or pamphlet
  is free from doctrinal or moral error. No implication is contained therein
  that those who grant the* imprimatur *agree with the contents or
  statements expressed.*

Scripture quotations are taken from the *Revised Standard Version of the Bible*,
Catholic edition, © 1965 and 1966 by the Division of Christian Education of the
National Council of the Churches of Christ in the USA, and are used by permission.

Library of Congress Cataloging-in-Publication Data
Dajczer, Tadeusz.
  [Tajemnica wiary. English]
  The mystery of faith : meditations on the Eucharist / Tadeus Dajczer ; [translated
by Artur Polit].
    p. cm.
  ISBN 978-1-55725-686-7
  1. Lord's Supper—Catholic Church—Meditations. I. Title.
  BX2235.D3513 2009
  234'.163—dc22   2009037265

10 9 8 7 6 5 4 3 2 1

Published in North America in 2009 by Paraclete Press
Brewster, Massachusetts
www.paracletepress.com
Printed in the United States of America

CONTENTS

FOREWORD BY
STANISŁAW CARDINAL DZIWISZ
METROPOLITAN ARCHBISHOP OF KRAKÓW

Unlike many books on the Eucharist, *The Mystery of Faith* focuses on our personal openness to this sacrament and our disposition to receiving graces flowing from it. The Eucharist operates both by God's action (*ex opera operato*) and through our co-operation (*ex opere operantis*).

Salvation comes through Jesus Christ, yet this salvation needs to be completely made real in each of us. Our Lord Jesus becomes truly present on the altar so as to enable His saving grace to achieve union with us. The valid and fruitful sacrament of Eucharist is the work of Christ himself but connected with responses from individual Christians. Without our faithful cooperation and collaboration with grace, Holy Communion will not be fruitful.

Usually books on the Eucharist speak of the action of Jesus by power of the Holy Spirit and His words (*ex opere operato*). By the power of these words—not the faith of priest or people—God really becomes present on the altar. Yet the fruits of His redeeming presence depend on the disposition both in holding and receiving the Eucharist (*ex opere operantis*). Graces which flow from the Real Presence do not spiritually force their way into us. "Behold, I stand and knock"—says God (cf. Rev. 3:20). He is never an uninvited guest.

What then are we to do so that the door is open for His coming under the appearances of bread and wine? What obstacles do we have to remove? This is exactly what *The Mystery of Faith* deals with in an unusually deep and simultaneously simple manner. The book shows how to open oneself to the presence of God alive both on the altar and in the tabernacle and how not to impede grace.

To become filled we need to be empty; to be fed we need to be hungry.

The Mystery of Faith invites us to see if there is actually a hunger for God in us, a hunger for Eucharist. It inspires us to attempt deeper contact with this sacrament in faith and love. After all, Christ always unfailingly wishes to pour His love into us. It is so easy to be closed to it. Then we not only do not receive the grace but, what is worse, it may happen that—as St. Paul says—in receiving the body and the blood of Christ—we are eating and drinking judgment upon ourselves (cf. 1 Cor. 11:29).

The Mystery of Faith opens deeper spaces for contact with the living God. To discover what is so very special about this book we have not only to read it but to pray with it. Its interior richness is amazing. For today's people taken up with worldly pursuits, it can become an unusual spiritual treasure. For those of us for whom contact with the holiest of the sacraments has become routine or stale, it will really make us sit up and think.

"The presence of Jesus in the tabernacle," writes John Paul II, "must be a kind of *magnetic pole* attracting an ever greater number of souls enamored of him, ready to wait patiently to hear his voice and as it were, to sense the beating of his heart."* *The Mystery of Faith* helps contemporary men and women to relate with increasing faith to the Blessed Sacrament and

---

* Apostolic Letter, *Mane Nobiscum Domine*, 18.

eventually to fall in love with God, to hear the beating of the eucharistic heart of Jesus.

Along with the author, my ardent wish is that the reader may find help in this book towards a deeper adoration and love of Him who incomprehensibly, daily, comes to us on the altar and stays with us in the tabernacle.

Metropolitan of Kraków

This **IS MY BODY**

IN THE TEXT YOU WILL FIND THE AUTHOR OFTEN WRITES IN THE FIRST PERSON. HE DOES THIS TO COMMUNICATE MOST EFFECTIVELY, NOT TO REVEAL HIS OWN INNER LIFE.

INTRODUCTION

The Church speaks of the universal call to holiness,[1] and this call means the challenge to each and every one of us towards having an interior life. Sacramental and interior life are deeply interdependent. On the one hand, sacramental life offers us objective contact with the saving grace of our Lord Jesus Christ. On the other, to achieve sanctity it is not enough to be present at Mass and receive His eucharistic body. We need to embrace this interiorly with faith and the humility that is the basis of the three theological virtues.[2]

The Eucharist is still the undiscovered land, the unknown world. Wanting to live the Eucharist, we need to hear the voice of grace that encourages: Set your foot on the undiscovered land, take the first, second,

---

[1] Cf. *Catechism of the Catholic Church*, 2013f.

[2] The theological virtues are faith, hope, and love.

and third step and He will lead you on. He, your God, who by rising from the dead has overcome all obstacles, now wants to introduce you to this stunning truth that is regularly occurring on our altars.

By the act of faith (which is a grace both of invitation and response) I can communicate with God who comes out to meet me in the Eucharist.

Once I have discovered this amazing world of God's personal earthly presence with us, I have the opportunity to become so taken up with it that I will be pulled towards the mystery of His very being. He said he wouldn't leave us orphans. He is true to His word, even more than I ever imagined. I am with Him in a different age with the advantage of receiving so much more.

It is amazing that the Church has received this great gift, that I can become a contemporary of Jesus walking in the land of Palestine. There is no doubt that here on the altar something has changed so that the glorified Jesus is himself present. It is magnificent discovering His love that wants not only to be with me but much more to be inside me at every moment. This hidden redeeming presence remains constantly to communicate itself to me while my mind is illuminated by faith.

PART I

Faith Bowing Humbly

I often enter church in just the same way as walking down the road, getting in and out of my car, moving around the house, being in a shop, or in my workplace. Perhaps when I am inside I don't even realize that I am actually in church. When I move around God's house in this way, it doesn't even occur to me that I am being so worldly. Yet my preparation for the miracle, soon to take place on the altar, should be in my thoughts as soon as I set foot in church.

Sometimes at the beginning of Mass, I am not really thinking of the meaning of the Penitential Rite. I may even be late and not sufficiently appreciative of this outstanding event. Yet I need to remember that in my repentance, God becomes present with His grace insofar as I am growing in the humility that makes the necessary space for eucharistic graces. By being late and inattentive, I miss out on these precious gifts.

As the Liturgy of the Word commences, I need to ponder the words. Perhaps because I'm familiar with what I hear, especially the Gospels, or perhaps because the readings of the Old Testament or the Epistles may be difficult to understand, I may switch off my mind and then God's grace may not touch me. If I automatically and thoughtlessly respond, "Thanks be to God," perhaps it is not a real act of faith. Surely, the words I just heard couldn't have been the **living word of God** for me. This Word shouldn't be just what was once written down in days gone by, but words sown into my heart here and now.

I need to realize that the eucharistic celebration rises to God gradually, leads toward the great event that is going to take place on the altar. Once the Liturgy of the Eucharist begins, I may not be aware that at the Preface I am getting near the central moment when our eucharistic God becomes **actually present**. This central moment is when the priest bends and starts slowly pronouncing the words of consecration. "The moment when the Lord comes down and transforms bread and wine to become his Body and Blood cannot fail to stun, to the very core of their being, those who participate in the Eucharist by faith and prayer."[1]

Do I realize that by the power of the Holy Spirit, in the reiteration of Christ's words, the greatest miracle in the world is taking place? At the very moment that I am kneeling I may not realize that at this moment the very posture of bending the knee is a special prayer of adoration. Yet this gesture helps make me small not just in the gesture but within. The liturgical sign of kneeling can prompt my consciousness, inspiring ever deepening faith.

Fatima not only means the Marian apparitions, but also the extraordinary message included in eucharistic visions. From the **big host drops of blood are flowing down into the cup.** The mighty **angel** bows deeply before the host, touches the ground with his forehead in deepest worship. His whole attitude expresses **the most profound adoration**. The children of Fatima, shaken by the force of God's presence, so intense that it almost consumes and annihilates them, receive God— the Body of Christ. The majestic might of God present in

---

[1] Joseph Cardinal Ratzinger, *The Spirit of the Liturgy*; San Francisco: Ignatius Press, 2000, 213.

the Eucharist lasts for so long that their senses become as if suspended.[2]

As I realize all of this, I am speechless seeing the inadequacy of my adoration before God's grandeur coming down onto the altar. He who governs this world is actually present. He who is Alpha and Omega of human history wants to unite himself with me in a measure that is beyond my normal capacity. This God adored by multitudes of angels comes to me as love, the redeeming One, the eucharistic One to give me everything, to fulfil me abundantly. To delight me with himself so that even I, so much immersed in this world, do not want anything else, but only His eucharistic love.

---

[2] Cf. *Fatima in Lucia's Own Words* (*Sister Lucia's Memoirs*, 1–4), Fátima, Portugal: Secretariado dos Pastorinhos, 2000.

Your Participation
Is the Way

My participation in the Eucharist is the way of opening up to God. God in the Eucharist wishes to fill me with His redemptive graces. This is truly amazing and unique but dependent on my humble openness to receive Him, on my **disposition** for receiving grace. My personal, humble attitude needs to be vitally united with God's descent into me not just while the Liturgy lasts but in my whole life.

My interior conversion affects every aspect of my daily vision, of how I view the world. And so, even though the same people and things are all around me, I now see them quite differently.

Yet there is a mysterious paradox: The more I need faith, the less I see it in me; but the more I see how I need faith, the less I know where to look for it. Actually this isn't so surprising since faith is a new dimension to human life. Moreover it is even more difficult as it doesn't belong to the natural. Faith is supernatural. It is God's dimension in me.

The impact of what is visible strongly tempts me to forget the Invisible. I am so engrossed in earthly life that I find it difficult to get beyond and think about this other world.

I am looking at the world You are continually creating. At the same time You are hiding Your creative powers so it seems that in human terms, all things were made by themselves. It was the same with the chosen people. You led them through the desert, surrounding them by the ceaseless miracle of manna falling to protect those You love against famine. You quenched their thirst with water from the rock. You destroyed the walls of Jericho. It was You who conquered the Promised Land for them. Still amid such miracles, the chosen people came to believe they did not need You. They thought they did it themselves by their own ingenuity and strength. They took every opportunity to leave You and serve some idol.

Is it so very different with me? You are always so brilliantly disguised so that it seems to me that grace is not there at all. You love my freedom and hate forcing me so much that no one can hide better than You. I sometimes even think that Your grace is mine because You are so well hidden. Only in the light of faith do I see that it is You who have been working in me all the time.

You want me to ask, even beg, for the grace of growing faith when my senses and my mind do not tell me anything. You wish, thanks to this light, that I try to see the adoring angel as in the Fatima event. You wish me to join the adoring angel who is completely captivated by Your acting in the Eucharist. You want Your presence to captivate me too as You, our infinite God, are worthy of unending glory.

I am not happy with being unable to see God on the altar. I feel like crying out: "Lord that I may see!" I am like the blind man in Jericho. I cannot remain indifferent before this mystery that is so much worshipped by the angel. Through the apparition, it is as if he wanted to tell me to do the same thing, at least to try.

It is very difficult to believe. Yet faith urges me forward to discover this extraordinary God who both reveals and hides himself so perfectly. He loves me yet He is invisible. Without faith I would despair. I am unaware that He is so close to rescue me from any threat. I do not need to fear anything. I am coming to You in an incredible way. You go ahead, and you make me walk in the footsteps You have left just for me.

LIKE THE PRODIGAL SON

"To prepare ourselves to celebrate the sacred mysteries, let us call to mind our sins." This is what I hear frequently at Mass in the Introductory Rites. I am standing before God trying to realize how important it is for me to acknowledge that I am a sinner. Without this my heart cannot be purified. No way can my hardheartedness be softened and my purification take place unless I open myself up. Unless I admit my sinfulness, a grace-preventing obstacle remains.

One kind of hardheartedness chooses the way of the elder brother in the parable of the prodigal son. But then if I do not repent, I resemble the hardheartedness of the younger one who walked out on his father prior to returning to him.

"We are all prodigal."[1] I am driving my car while taking note of the people I pass en route. I am thinking they are also prodigal sons and daughters. Because of original sin we all share the same wounded, confused human nature. There is a barrier of self-sufficiency inducing me to reject my need for God and His eucharistic presence. Many of us prodigal ones go to Sunday Mass without realizing that in practice we are living as though we have no need for God and Mass. Often we go just out of a sense of duty. Yet this attitude makes me nothing other than my own god. For close union with the almighty One, I need to become aware of my prodigality just like the son in the parable.

I am on my way to church to attend Mass. I am not thinking about God. However, I am thinking that since I'm going, I must have some belief. My religious life is mostly going through rituals, now and then passionately. I am just like the people of Nazareth or Capernaum. The people of the first wanted to kill Jesus, the people of the other did not trust his words. Unless I change radically, I will never discover Him in the eucharistic reality. The Eucharist will just remain one of my rituals.

---

[1] John Paul II, *Reconciliatio et paenitentia*, 5.

The people of Nazareth or Capernaum followed religious observances but they had never chosen Jesus. Strong interior barriers blocked them from belief. It was about the people of Capernaum that Jesus uttered the woes of Matthew 11:22.

To choose Jesus is to allow grace to crush the barriers in my heart. Those big barriers of trust in my own abilities and self-confidence need to collapse. If my trust is in myself, I am self-centered, not Jesus- or Eucharist-centered.

How can God infuse His love into me if I am only full of self-confidence? This self-centeredness is a huge barrier to the infusion of His eucharistic love. It needs to collapse so that I can allow myself to be transformed by eucharistic love.

There are three turning points in that famous parable of the prodigal son. The first is when the son leaves his father's house. The second is the breakdown of his former life and the crisis so deep that he had never experienced before. That was when he had to take up pig farming, didn't get paid and was starving. The third turning point is when he is returning to his father who is all love.

Each event inspires a special consideration. In the first, there is the self-sufficiency in his desire to leave his father until the moment of his crisis. The second is the return to his father's house. He is full of uncertainty and some hidden human hope. Finally comes the unexpected enlightening astonishment that must have made him speechless—that unexpectedly positive, warm, loving, welcome home.

All of us prodigal sons and daughters resist God's grace. I cannot believe in the eucharistic presence unless I believe I am prodigal. Insofar as I learn to believe this, God's loving presence can grow in me. I cannot start my return to the loving Father unless I am convinced I am a needy prodigal. However, to start the way back I need a trial of faith so that I realize in some small or big way that I am helpless. The situation will remind us of that critical moment when that famous prodigal son becomes a pig farmer.

Every one of us is prodigal. Human life is a continual departure from God. It needs to be a continual return to Him. Even if I do not suffer pangs of conscience, the wound of original sin constantly makes itself felt. In my life there are always two directions—"from" and "to" the Father. That means conversion needs to be a regular event in my Christian life. "Conversion is never once and for all but is a process, an interior journey through the whole of life."[2]

To believe in the Lord's presence on the altar means I need to remember I am prodigal. It is not easy because my constant self-satisfaction keeps telling me that although I am prodigal, I am already safely in the Father's arms. Yet the prodigal son had to leave before he returned into those arms.

He may not have been so far away that he couldn't be in touch at times. Maybe father and son were actually in close contact. They may even have embraced, but the unconscious attitude of the prodigal was always dormant within him until that great return.

The younger son could have been totally convinced that he loved his father. We often lead very superficial sorts of lives. Living on the surface, he didn't find out what was actually deeply hidden within him. It is easier not to discover that inner twilight zone because then I can live comfortably self-satisfied. It is very pleasant when everything is well between my father and me. Appearances are highly convenient.

---

[2] Benedict XVI, General Audience, Ash Wednesday, February 21, 2007.

Presumably the prodigal son had to leave because of this kind of falsehood. His father allowed him to go in order to regain him, not superficially with many exterior appearances, but more deeply. The surgeon has to cut through tissue so he can heal. When God wants to offer me the gift of the Eucharist, He has to remove what lies on the surface through trials. Sometimes they are painful. I don't deeply believe I am prodigal and constantly departing so I don't believe I should be constantly returning. I don't believe because in the depth of my being there is a resistance to healing grace. I never dream that my ever patient eucharistic Father is waiting for me.

Of course I am not bound to stumble or fall. But if I am not open to the idea that I am prodigal, I shall have no experience of that love. Like St. Thérèse of Lisieux, I need to see my twilight zone through the light of faith. That great saint found God forgave her more than Mary Magdalene,[3] If I don't think like that, I will have to become another Mary Magdalene. I will have to become a pig farmer; however, God does not want

---

[3] "I . . . know that Jesus has *forgiven me more* than *St. Mary Magdalene* since He forgave me *in advance* by preventing me from falling." The *Story of a Soul: The Autobiography of St. Thérèse of Lisieux*; Washington D.C.: ICS Publications, 1976; 83.

this, because the way of a prodigal son who has fallen so low is accompanied by the way of a father's loving tears and sorrow.

I realize that I should listen intently to the words of the Introductory Rites. The encouragement is there: Let us acknowledge that we are sinners—I need to accept with faith that I am prodigal so that I will really experience the mercy that will pour into the participants of the sacrifice of the cross as the eucharistic celebration makes it present.

Graces from the eucharistic altar flow into me insofar as I am humble, in the measure that I understand that I will never manage my life without God. I need His indescribable love. I need Jesus in the Eucharist to make up for my poverty of having no personal, supernatural good within me. If my humility is beginning to reach the depth of the humility of the prodigal son, I will experience how much I am loved. Just like the prodigal, I need the fulfilment of Jesus in the Eucharist. God **gives Himself completely** only to those who are **desperately needy**.

As Background

In the attitude of the tax collector I admit that You are still too little in my life. Everything around me attracts me, absorbs me, involving me in the sphere of its actions as if beyond this world nothing else existed at all. By this attitude, I am far away from You. The horizon of what I see is hidden by the river of sensations I am looking for, to which I am surrendering myself, in which I am losing myself. These sensations and feelings have nothing to do with redemption. Likewise they have nothing to do with the Eucharist that makes that redemption present.

Isn't there a kind of a drama going on in my life so that You are actually pushed to the background of my thoughts and actions? You are only in the background, not in the forefront. I push You far away from me. I may be doing something for You, but in fact I am not very much interested in You. You are always second, third, or even tenth in my scale of importance. After all, I have so many friends, members of my family, so many urgent matters. If I work it out, will I say You are seventeenth? So this makes You very much in the background.

Because of this scenario, I need You so much. You have to come to me today and keep coming all the time. You are really present in the Eucharist. Chasing after an elevated place, courting the avarice of possessing, searching for pleasure and bodily comfort—all these things will destroy me.

I can still see that You are only in the background. Even worse, I prefer not to remove You from this background. I need it like that. I would even feel bad without it. I keep You just in the background of my life, small enough not to disturb me in my commitments and pursuits.

How obstinate I am. Yet it is hidden in me. It is somewhere deep in my subconsciousness. It is unmistakably there. I am ashamed to spell it out, but the fact is I feel good keeping You small like that. You fit just nicely in my scheme of things. You keep just where You are. I like to be "normal," and if You were to get big and great in my life, there would be an upheaval. I would not be able to cope. I can't allow that. That just won't do at all. I would not have my peace of mind, the comfort that's granted to me by the compromises I've made.

Despite all this, grace still breaks through to me. More and more I can see that I need You. I need You so much. You are my redeeming God. You have come to sinners like me. That is why You come in the Eucharist to save me from my obstinacy against which I am so helpless.

If You are in the background, I am big and important in the whole scenario. I am sitting on a really big throne. I am actually on a throne with God in the background. The radiance is coming from that background giving a new dimension to everything. A job is not a job any more. It is a dedication. Human relationships are almost radiant. Even my thoughts if they have You for their background, take on a brilliantly new significance.

Yet You can see that in reality it is You I desperately need—really desperately. By treating You subconsciously as the background I am actually destroying myself, my family, my friends, the world. This truth I discover in the act of contrition is so transfixing that I am now racing to You with even greater passion. With the attitude of the tax collector I am crying out, "God present in the Eucharist, save me!"

How perverse this all is—the apostolic work for You may be very reassuring; I may get a lot of satisfaction from this work. After all, I convert people. I speak about You so much. I am like a sort of hero the way I work. Yet this is only because of You. If You disappeared from the background, then my whole missionary activity would make no sense. So You have to be in the background as this is what makes my apostolate, my whole life sensible. It gives me this unusual peace that I convince myself I am living for extraordinary things. I do it—with You in the background!

Even the important matter of winning souls for You is contaminated. Yet the fact that You show me this contamination should be a great light and grace for me. Because then my crying out for You, God in the Eucharist, becomes stronger and stronger, and my need to cling to You gets stronger too. The nearness of Your merciful love will, I believe, save me. Moreover, I see that the problem of the background is beginning to show itself differently. What I used to see as background was all confusion, immersed in my ego. I now clearly see that no one can help me. I only have You. The more dangerously confused I am, the more Your eucharistic mercy spills into me because You are love itself.

I need You, my God, I need you so very much in Your eucharistic mercy. You want to forgive me all this. You want to save me. You want to sanctify me. Despite my confused obstinacy, despite my immersion in egocentric desires, You are in love with me. You are overlooking my selfishness. The more You can grant me Your forgiveness, the greater Your glory.

In Your love, You only need my contrition and increasing faith.

God, working in the Eucharist by the power of the Holy Spirit, immerse my poor soul in the waters of contrition. Show me it is really not worth focusing on myself, because I was Your special choice even before You made me.

You have made the whole world for me. When You are speaking to me from the altar, I shall know better and better to open myself to Your love that wants to revive and transform me. Transform me to the point where the world is in the background so that You become the center of my life. According to the faith I receive in and through our Church, I want the Eucharist to be the source and the sense of my spiritual life. I want You to lead me by my faith. I want to be led to sanctity.

WHEN GOD IS CLOSEST

We should never tire of saying that the Eucharist communicates our redemption. After all, on the altar there is the continuous saving work of our divine merciful one, always craving that I might seize the most of the fruits of His saving passion. Continuous redemption on the world's altars means redemption of my personal evil. I need to see my evil in the light of faith. I need to see that God is responding to my faith and contrition. He even uses my evil so that His mercy can more abundantly flow right into me.

I am never alone with my fear, despair, disappointment, or a crisis involving accepted authority. Any kind of difficult situation is a trial of faith. I may feel alone and helpless in the face of such trials. Yet the truth is really quite different, paradoxically different. In these highly difficult moments, God is actually closest to me. In times of huge sexual temptations, Christ says to St. Catherine of Siena: "I have never been so close to you as in this moment." In such moments, God is simply just waiting for me. He is waiting for me to discover the value and treasure of the Eucharist. In every temptation, crisis, fear, or moment of despair, He wants to embrace and transform me by this redeeming sacrament.

Crises may touch me personally, others, or whole communities. Many times in the past when such crises arose in the Church and Christian faith diminished, it looked like the end. Yet the Church cannot perish. The Church will endure until the end of time, as our Savior promises. The gates of hell will not prevail (cf. Mt 16:18). The crisis of faith among the faithful has sometimes spread so widely that to those of lesser faith it might have seemed that it was not a crisis of human belief but of the Church itself. It looked as though everything had already collapsed.

I cannot imagine what St. Joan of Arc thought as she was being tried by a Church tribunal. She experienced deeply engulfing darkness during her trial. She counted this as her Gethsemane, her Calvary. Her faith endured. She didn't confuse bishops for the Church itself. Standing before the judging Church tribunal which she knew wanted to sentence her to death, she said "The Church is Christ."[1]

I should not have total belief in people, even if they are bishops. If I do, on noting their failures, I may be in danger of a serious spiritual crisis. It is wrong to put all my hope in holy spiritual directors, holy priests, or bishops. All my hope should be in Christ on the altar by the power of the Holy Spirit as He shows forth His death on the cross. I need to have complete trust in Him, not in erring men and women.

St. Francis of Assisi was unaffected by the evil of his time that flourished like raging flood waters. The bulls of Pope Innocent III, condemning the most shocking abuses of usury, business corruption, gluttony, intemperance, and debauchery, highlight a very gloomy picture of the Church in the twelfth century. Against a background of a big decline in morality, there were many fanatical and aggressive heresies which seriously undermined European Christianity. The Church also suffered from itinerant preachers ceaselessly criticizing wealth-craving clergy who were compared

---

[1] Quoted in *Catechism of the Catholic Church*, 795.

with examples of evangelical poverty. In tradition there is the story of Pope Innocent III having a dream (not too historically certain) that the Lateran Basilica, symbolic of the Church, was collapsing.[2] The situation was saved by the Poor Man of Assisi. Indeed, the sanctity of one man changed history, restoring the damaged faith of the people.

When I see that everything around me is collapsing, increasing evil and darkness that may engulf me, I need to remember the words of St. Paul: "where sin increased, grace abounded all the more." (Rom. 5:20) If I see my personal selfishness or egoism in those around me, I can see it as an opportunity to look for the solution in the one place I can find it. I need to turn to the one who loves me and unceasingly transmits His redeeming graces on the altar. In my difficulties, He is here and now closer to me than ever.

The chosen people's forty years of wandering in the desert mirrors humankind's journey towards God. It is an image of my history too. I can detect in it some of my own temptations to doubt in the face of what seems

---

[2] Still today the Latin inscription can be seen there: *Mater et caput omnium eccelsiarum.* "Mother and head of all churches."

to be overpowering. For Moses, who led the wandering during this time, it sometimes seemed that everything was falling apart. He felt as though his life was one big failure. Perseverance seemed to bring him to the breaking point. The Bible sums up his extraordinary perseverance: "He endured as seeing Him who is invisible." (Heb. 11:27)

I need to be reminded that everything is taking place according to God's will or at least with His consent. After all, He foresees it all from the beginning and decides how opposition to His will can best be utilized. "Wicked men," writes St. Augustine, "do many things contrary to God's will; but so great is His wisdom and power, that all things which seem adverse to His purpose do still tend towards those just and good ends and issues which He himself has foreknown."[3] And somewhere else: "For almighty God . . . because he is supremely good, would never allow any evil whatsoever to exist in his works if he were not so all-powerful and good as to cause good to emerge from evil itself."[4]

---

[3] *De civitate Dei*, 22,2,1.

[4] *Opus imperf. Contra Julianum*, Lib. 5, nr. 60; cf. also *Catechism of the Catholic Church*, 311.

Augustine's words are shocking: "What is done in opposition to His will does not defeat His will. . . . God accomplishes some of His purposes, which of course are all good, through the evil desires of wicked men."[5] Earth may be shaking in its foundations, hurricanes may devastate our land, authorities may fall, our trusted leaders may be compromising, and yet I don't need to worry a bit. At first I may be full of anxiety that those I trusted could be like that. Yet as I listen to Jesus I hear: Nothing is impossible for me. I can turn every evil into an asset which will bear fruit outshining even my greatest glory.

If He can bring greater glory from that evil, what of the glory of this great eucharistic miracle? Just as He can transform bread and wine into His body and blood, He can certainly turn the biggest evil into something so good that His glory will be dazzling before me and the world.[6] Perhaps deep down I will hear what Nathaniel

---

[5] *The Enchiridion; Or, on Faith, Hope and Love,* translated by Professor J. F. Shaw, Chapter 100–101. [*Enchiridion de fide, spe et caritate,* 26, 100–101 PL 40, 236.] Available online at *http://www.leaderu.com/cyber/books/augenchiridion/enchiridiontoc.html.*

[6] "From the greatest moral evil ever committed—the rejection and murder of God's only Son, caused by the sins of all men—God, by his grace that 'abounded all the more,' brought the greatest of goods: the glorification of Christ and our redemption." (*Catechism of the Catholic Church,* 312).

heard: "You are going to see greater things than that. You will see heaven open and the angels of God ascending and descending over the Son of man." (Jn. 1:50–51)

Everything is included in God's plan. Of course it is secret at present. Nobody knows for how long. Nobody knows how it will all work out. Here and now it may seem to be really terrifying, and yet through His redemptive power present on the altar, astonishing results can emerge. Although I don't always see it, I am always loved. The infinite one who created the skies above, He who is love alone, has everything in hand.

I sometimes wonder how the incomprehensible love of Jesus connects with the murky sin within us; how come there is a wave of murky sin flooding the world almost from the beginning of our existence? Could it really be something completely useless for God's omnipotence? Is it possible that weakness, helplessness, and evil were only there to crush us without a deeper meaning? Could evil only be the defeat of love, the denial of God who is love? Through faith I discover that the power of the eucharistic sacrifice can convert these murky, sinful things into a great asset. From that asset a flood of yet unknown graces is to be born. *Si comprehendis, non est Deus*—"if you understand him, he is not God." as Pope Benedict XVI quotes from St. Augustine in the encyclical *Deus caritas est.*[7]

These thoughts inspire me to have the optimism to see that through faith **all will be well**. These thoughts inspire the peace and joy which can only flow from discovering the love present in the Eucharist. God wants to redeem everything. So he allows what is bad so that He can make it completely different. "Behold, I make all things new." (Rev. 21:5)

He loves me as I am. He doesn't look to see how bad I am or may be. This is not as important for Him as the fact that He always loves me. He can cope with dirty sinfulness. For Him I am always the most beautiful because I am His beloved. This becomes my source of peace and joy which will increase the more my faith increases.

When I try to look at evil with faith, or if I fall into it, however bad the situation may be, God in His unfathomable love can amazingly remedy and improve things. His is a love that can always bring good out of evil. It is hard to resist His power when I gaze at Him. Looking at

---

[7] Benedict XVI, *Deus caritas est*, 38.

Him with faith, I actually participate in His great victory for good. If God snatches good from that evil, it will just bear fruit to His greater glory. The downfall of the powerful shows that it is not people who make history. God alone is the master. In fact, He is the only one. Exactly in these seemingly hopeless moments, God elevates His Church by raising up extraordinary saints whose sanctity inspires religious revival. So an apparent failure turns into a new resurrection.

PART II

THE SACRAMENT
OF THE PRESENT MOMENT

There's often some conflict in my daily life. On the one hand I want to go to Mass and find time to pray, on the other I have many things to do. I am often rather stressed. I need to learn to cope. I am frequently feverishly active. I feel God is far from me. I am sometimes a prisoner of my emotions. Pressures frequently overwhelm me. God seems to be miles away.

St. Edith Stein had similar pressures. At times she had very taxing difficulties and problems or a feeling of helplessness. With great faith she wrote: "I am doing my best. I derive courage constantly from the tabernacle."[1]

When it seems as though there is no time for prayer, Blessed Elisabeth of the Holy Trinity says we can learn

---

[1] *Life in a Jewish Family: Her Unfinished Autobiographical Account* (*Collected Works of Edith Stein*, Vol. 1); Washington D.C.: ICS Publications, 1999; Letter 217.

by faith that we can pray with at least the attention we give to events, meetings, joyful or unpleasant things. There is a temptation to consider these events in isolation. I think I can go to the Lord later. This daily running around is a sort of disturbance for me. It is a threat to my union with God. Blessed Elisabeth speaks with clarity on the issue. She shows that that is where faith needs to be intimately involved. Thus every coincidence, every happening, every suffering, every joy becomes **a sacramental meeting with God**.

The word "sacrament" refers to every small daily event in which we allow the influence of God's love. It is reminiscent of the expression "sacrament of the present moment" used by Father Jean-Pierre de Caussade. The sacrament of the present moment or living with the grace of the moment opposes haste. By haste I live in the future. God's presence is now. God is not in the future or the past. He is just present now.

I don't often realize how much haste disturbs my journey towards the invisible one. Haste dominates the desire so that I am overtaken by the event and over-anxious to get what I want. So much of me is nervously frenetic, feverishly making plans with hectic effort to get a move on, racing hastily towards my goal.

This kind of activity simply impedes my discovery of eucharistic love.

Perhaps I should begin by slowing down every step I take. Every moment, as Father Jean-Pierre de Caussade writes, is a time when I can receive God's love. I can only assimilate this love if I let go of feverish activity, frenzied anxiety, my attempts to put my personal seal on everything I do. That is the way to be really prayerful. It is enough for me to slow down the pace of my activity so that I make way for God's presence. That is how I prepare the way for peaceful, eucharistic love.

If my words about God are not immersed in a sort of silence as they are uttered, they come from a godless mouth. What is more, no one will listen to me. To hear God we need silence like Elijah on Mount Horeb.

When I am pressed for time, slowing down itself can be an act of faith. With an activity that is more paced, I can begin to pray. I do it for Him. This slower activity is a proper preparation for my reception of Him in the Eucharist.

When I drive a car, I try to pray in the act of driving itself, just by touching the steering wheel or the pedals. I will somehow bring God into that activity. It is enough that it is being done differently, and on account of this one who is waiting for me with an abundance of eucharistic graces. Every attempt to slow down or do it differently becomes an act of faith as it is directed to this one who craves nothing more than continuously to be communicating His grace on me.

"My daughter, I too came down from heaven out of love for you; I lived for you, I died for you, and I created the heavens for you," said the Lord Jesus to St. Faustina.[2] Yet don't these words also apply to me if I accept His mercy just like St. Faustina? He also descended from heaven out of love for me. He lived for me. He died for me. He created the heavens for me. This is God's amazing love as if He were talking to me personally: for you I am coming onto the altar. It is for you that I am bringing about this miraculous transformation.

I am sometimes tempted to think it is all very well for St. Faustina with her special vocation, but that is not for me. I don't want it. Yet doesn't that reveal a hidden resistance on my part to God's grace? After all, it is He who chooses. Didn't He choose the twelve apostles, who were just ordinary people?

---

[2] *Diary of Saint Faustina Kowalska: Divine Mercy In My Soul*; Stockbridge, MA: Marian Press, 2007; 334.

Slowing down involves coming into silence. Within this silence, I can discover God. I can only live the sacrament of the present moment by this silence.

This sacrament discovered in daily life leads to the Blessed Sacrament, the sacrament that is the peak of Christian life. We can say that since the Eucharist is the sacrament of faith, then everything that holds back the growth of faith in me holds back the flow of redeeming grace flowing either in holding the Eucharist or by God's presence in the tabernacle.

Faith means seeing what is invisible. My participation in the Eucharist is a prayer of humble faith. It draws me into humbly exercising more constant loving attentiveness to the invisible one. He is **really present** under species of bread and wine. Yet is it so easy to stand by in loving attentiveness? My prayer during the Eucharist, the prayer of humble faith, is actually generally distracted because until now I have not clung to God. If I am completely preoccupied by something during the day or totally immersed in something, then it is not possible for me to be focused when I am coming into church or when Jesus appears on the altar. My attitude during the Eucharist reflects my divided life in which I so often forget God. The reality is that everything that happens to me during the day revives when I am trying to pray before the altar.

I am not only often preoccupied by events, I am also taken up with my vivid imagination. As St. Teresa of Avila says: "Since it sees itself alone, the war it wages is something to behold—how it strives to disturb everything. As for me, I find the memory tiresome and abhorrent. I often beseech the Lord to take it away during these periods if it is going to bother me so much. . . . The only remedy I have, having tired myself out for many years, is . . . to pay no more attention to the memory than one would to a madman."[3]

So how can I learn concentration? I need humbly to ask for it and often to practice greater concentration throughout the day. This concentration means living more carefully, more slowly, not hurrying towards a future constructed from mental patterns under the influence of something in my past life. The rule is: do whatever you do without overstretching yourself, not expecting to finish what you have begun.

---

[3] *The Collected Works of St. Teresa of Avila*, Vol. 1; Washington, D.C.: ICS Publications, 1976; 155–156. The text of endnote 4 therein: "She refers to the memory and the imagination without distinguishing them from each other."

However we shall not fulfil our expectations either during prayer or at Mass. We are never free from distractions. So I shall be continually beginning it but never actually finishing. Searching is finding and finding is searching, teaches St. Gregory of Nyssa.[4]

God is silence. When I try to be still, pushing my way towards the invisible one, I am entering the extraordinary circle of His amazing, saving, eucharistic presence. With this He will be embracing me more and more.

---

[4] St. Gregory of Nyssa, *Homiliae In Canticum*, 8 PG 44,941 C.

IN THE SEARCH
OF OUR HIDDEN GOD

M ost of St. Benedict Labre's[1] contemporaries had
a pretty low opinion of him. Human pride
emphasizes what is great, wise, and bright. He was
turned down by the Carthusians, the Trappists, and the
Cistercians. Nobody wanted him. This is precisely the sort
of trial of faith that we may look at in a different way.

Through rejection I can draw into myself: I can
focus on people's nastiness, or I can see it in the light
of faith. After all, if I deepen in eucharistic devotion,
being a castaway can fill me with the one who can give
me everything.

---

[1] St. Benedict Labre (born 1748 in France—died 1783 in Rome). Not accepted for a monastic life, he went on pilgrimages to Italy, Germany, and
Spain; from 1774 he stayed in Rome begging in the Colosseum. He distin-
guished himself by his special love for the Blessed Sacrament, by humility,
love of poverty, and prayer. The alms he received he shared with those
poorer than himself. He was beatified in 1861, and canonized in 1881.

St. Benedict could have gotten completely lost if he had been wanted. We all greatly need to be wanted. As his contemporaries didn't want him, God in the Eucharist became everything to him. God became the overwhelming light of his life. The compelling enlightenment of our mysteriously hidden eucharistic God became so strong for him that his life developed into that of a wanderer in search of the Eucharist. He went from church to church to adore wherever there was exposition of the Blessed Sacrament. Failing that, he went where he could kneel and pray before a tabernacle.

The people of Rome referred to him as the beggar or the man wrapped up in the Gospel. He was utterly fulfilled by God's eucharistic love. The Blessed Sacrament was his pearl of great price for which he sold everything. Admittedly he didn't have much. Everybody looked down on him. Yet he sold what he did have. Instead he bought this priceless pearl, the discovery of God for whom he constantly looked on the altar or in the tabernacle. There he found all-embracing, unlimited love being the whole sense of his life. He never stopped wandering in pursuit of God, who loved him through and through.

Because he was unwanted, the truth of Christ's eucharistic presence meant everything to him. The more nobody wants me, the more I can experience Christ's wanting me. Who or what can outmeasure such treasure? This is the complete answer to every inhibition and wound, to that mysterious personal feeling of loneliness or sense of desertion. I gain a greater treasure that way.

So he learned from the one who always wanted him as the greatest pleasure for Himself that his vocation is to roam all over the place. After all, hadn't he been rejected by monasteries? Now his monastery became streets and roads. They all lead to the Eucharist. So he was able to become like this Jesus by whom he was so fascinated. In Him as pilgrim, he found outstanding treasure. Moreover he was able to follow this one who also had nowhere to rest his head. God wanted Him so much. "Foxes have holes and birds of the air have nests, but the Son of man has nowhere to lay his head." (Mt. 8:20)

What an unusual adventure following this amazing event in the life of Jesus by pursuing the master of the world, living in a sort of loneliness because I neglect to adore Him or to share my problems. In a variety of ways, He would like to give me everything leading to invisible reality now and for eternity. I cannot enter His

51

glory unless here and now I walk in His footsteps. The purpose of earthly life is to lead me to an ever deepening union with the eucharistic Jesus. In that way, the world becomes the way to union with eucharistic love.

The love I always discover in the Mass, I can find everywhere, whether I am under the spotlight or in the shadows. The master of the universe waits for me. He needs my presence.

Sometimes I think there is no place for me in this world. This is a great opportunity to find grace from the homeless God wandering on Palestinian soil. I think I have the right to turn to Him because He wants to tell me not to become lost, whether I live in a palace or in some poor shelter. To alert me, He calls out: "Look, I am changing everything fundamentally. There is no such safe place where you could settle down." Maybe my paradise will be destroyed by a cyclone, a storm, or a hurricane, shattering into oblivion every authority in which I have believed or on which I pinned my hopes while quite forgetting God. He utters terrifying words to those who put too much trust in clerical or lay authorities: "Thus says the Lord: Cursed is the man who trusts in man and makes flesh his arm, whose heart turns away from the Lord." (Jer. 17:5)

Isn't it better to walk in the streets like St. Benedict Labre looking for our hidden God instead of getting over-anxious as we try to escape from flooded territories or as we look for new authorities? Constantly searching for human assistance is, in effect, seeking perfection attributed to some personal or collective authority.

I could one day find myself a victim of a tsunami, earthquake, or some material or psychological catastrophe. Everything may fall apart. For St. Benedict Labre nothing could fall apart because his treasure couldn't be lost. It was because of this Gospel-based treasure that he wandered from church to church. He never stopped looking for that hidden presence. Jesus in the Eucharist was His heart's desire. I am full of anxiety. Without human assistance I feel I will die.

Maybe as I kneel before the tabernacle I will hear this gentle whisper of Jesus: You will not perish. I will protect you in your poverty or sense of loss. I will take you in my arms and embrace you so that you, homeless for whatever reason, finally find your true home in my heart. Just don't forget to call on Me day and night. Because without calling, somehow you appropriate to yourself this apartment in my house and you may lose it. You have to call constantly. I want you to be in touch.

Your calling may become the highest form of needing Me, the highest form of looking for Me. The paradox is that you have found Me, yet you constantly have to look for Me. May faith and hope and this real sense of security that St. Benedict found also take root in you. Benedict Labre found security in any place or on any rock where he rested his head.

No need for a pillow. A rock moved him closer to the one and only eucharistic love. That was it. God did it for him. Jesus in the Eucharist is sufficient for me too.

EUCHARIST GIVING BIRTH TO PRIESTS

As she saw a young nun looking after a sick girl, Mother Teresa of Calcutta said:

See this girl? Not long ago she came to us. She was unsettled. This morning I talked to her. I asked whether she would have noticed with what love and care the priest at Mass had touched Jesus under the appearances of bread and wine. I advised her to do the same whenever she is with the dying. I told her she would meet Jesus in the frail, sick and poor people for whom she cared. Not long after, she came to me and said "Mother, thank you. I have been touching Jesus for three hours." Now she is with Him.[1]

---

[1] Cf. *In the Silence of the Heart: Meditations by Mother Teresa of Calcutta*, compiled by Kathryn Spink, London: SPCK, 1983; 56.

Imagine you are standing by Mother Teresa in heaven and she asks: "Do you realize that at Mass when the priest adores the host under appearances of bread and wine, he is adoring Jesus?" She suggests you do the same when you are with a sick person at home, in the street or anywhere else. Likewise for the spiritually sick.

Perhaps these words of Mother Teresa of Calcutta will point you toward a priestly vocation. Priesthood viewed by faith is a truly remarkable sacrament in which God shines forth. Priests do the most important work of consecrating bread and wine in the sacrifice of the Mass and preaching the Good News. Maybe you will hear these words: I have chosen you and want you to look at these souls pining for God. In my name, you communicate redemption in the most sacred mysteries.

The Eucharist, looked at in deep faith, gives birth to the best priestly vocations. Because they come from eucharistic love, they are the best. Vocations arise from deep love of the Blessed Sacrament. Apply Mother Teresa's words. It could be that you will be called from Mass to touch dying souls with God's love. God wants nothing more from the priest than to communicate to dying souls the truth that **God does love you!**

When you see it, you will forget worldly pursuits to sacrifice yourself in this way. Is there anything more magnificent than following Christ who wants priestly witness in you coming from your eucharistic love?

If you strongly believe in this greatest miracle which by God's power takes place in the Mass, you will believe that faith works miracles and gathers crowds alive with His mysterious love. They will only want to live for this life of eucharistic love. That is because they will have found that life only makes sense in clinging to the one who wants to save our dying world and is sending you to help Him. Still there are so few, these sent ones, but you will come from the altar alive with God's glory in your heart. Your conversation will be different. It will be God himself pouring graces through you.

If you have received the glory of discovery of Eucharist, so you may desire to sacrifice your life for the Eucharist. Nothing could be better. The priest has blessed hands through distributing God's presence in the Blessed Sacrament. There is nothing more sacred than this. Seeing this through your hesitations, you will see its indescribable value.

In place of Christ, the priest holds the host. It is incredible that the priest is so close to God himself. This just shows God's crazy love because it is He who rules the entire world. You will raise God. You will be giving God to others. You will be repeating the words of Jesus himself. By the power of the Holy Spirit you will be a channel for the biggest miracle in the world.

Can you hold back from racing after this God who lets you hold Him in your palms for so long, letting you be close to Him rather like His Blessed Mother? Only by faith can you discover the invisible. Perhaps, like that angel's eucharistic vision, you will undergo a crisis in which God shows you the truth, scales will fall from your eyes, and you will see. Only in deep faith is it possible to see God on the altar. Before the glory of eternity, here and now there is power and infinite majesty.

PART III

INTERIOR SILENCE

Before Holy Communion I pray: Lord Jesus Christ, You have said: "I leave you peace, my peace I give you." (Jn. 14:27) As mentioned so much by St. John of the Cross, this peace comes to me through faith even when I am worn out. By faith I will find the infinitely powerful and loving Jesus in the Eucharist. In Him I will find rest. I will listen to His extraordinary words of love.

Faith is like a guide for the blind who leads and carries me to an unknown place where I find the hidden God.[1] Faith, as St. John of the Cross teaches, is darkness mixed with abandonment. Like the blind man, I have to trust the guide completely, following him by holding

---

[1] Cf. St. John of the Cross, *Spiritual Canticle*, I, 11.

his hand. Faith not only directs, it also strengthens our purpose.

If on the way to God I find the attractive pull of people and things too difficult to resist, God can help me by making these attractions less compelling through putting them into a darker region of my feelings. How does St. John of the Cross understand this darkness? In *The Ascent of Mount Carmel* he points out that the cloud which led the Israelites through the desert to the Promised Land was dark yet strangely providing light in the night (cf. Ex. 14:20).[2]

"Darkness" doesn't literally mean lack of light. The Lord can rearrange the emotional forces involved in excessively powerful relationships or over preoccupation with things. He can renew everything in a fresh, healthier kind of attraction so that I am no longer overwhelmed with excessively egocentric enthusiasm. He comforts me by a calming influence in any sense of loss. He can lead me by a dark tunnel into new light and life.

There is no doubt that my journey to God is liberating. By faith everybody and everything look different.

---

[2] Cf. *The Ascent of Mount Carmel*, II, 3, 4–5.

I grow in true liberation, free from excessive dependencies and fears. I grow in certainty that He is watching and guiding it all. The One who loves me so mysteriously comes onto the altar so that in faith, there is a close union.[3] His real presence. The presence of this one who loves.

What I call love and friendship are often like addictions to other humans. Such relationships frequently both support and oppress me. "Love causes equality and likeness," remarks St. John of the Cross, "and even brings the lover lower than the loved object."[4] Being over obsessed with another person impedes my vision of faith in this miracle on the altar. I have to make a choice. Either I will become controlled by my passions or have the liberation of deeper faith. "Thus says the Lord: Cursed is the man who trusts in man." (Jer. 17:5)

I may not realize that wherever I kneel in church, I always bring my own "altar" to the altar. This altar doesn't occupy space, but it is pretty full. It varies from person to person. It involves what in reality I am

---

[3] "He touches Christ, who believes in Christ," said St. Augustine in his 243rd Sermon.

[4] *The Ascent of Mount Carmel*, I, 4,4; in *The Collected Works of St. John of the Cross*, trans. by Kieran Kavanaugh and Otilio Rodriguez; Washington, D.C.: ICS Publications, 1991; 125.

consciously or unconsciously worshipping in my life. That altar is really what I place on the altar to adore.

I often speak of what I adore. "To adore" in any language does not imply trying to throw God from His throne. I use it out of habit. In a natural way, although almost unconsciously, I am relegating God, whom I should really adore, into the background.

The situation is odd because I can see the altar from my pew in church—but what do I actually see? Not the true altar but this one in my mind. I have brought it with me. It obscures the altar of the most holy sacrifice. I don't realize that I simply don't see it.

So the silence I try to have as I kneel before the tabernacle cannot be real. God wants to grant me a real liberation—not in the sense of choice between good and evil but in freedom from desires, from fears and obsessions. He wants to grant me true interior silence that is both freedom from hindrances and peace coming from union with Him. This one who grants me peace, frequently calms my sense of loss and loneliness.

The silence of faith leads to grace. This consists in quietening the passions and desires. It is about the silence of the will so that I have fewer and fewer yearnings. The less I pursue desires, the more I find peace.

God magnetizes the emotional forces into tranquil pathways free from clingy attachments. Instead my love is magnificently renewed.

In Holy Communion I unite myself with Jesus—or so it seems to me. But do I really unite myself with Him? He comes into my heart yet He finds it cluttered. I may find this hard to imagine. How many temporarily unused thrones are cluttering my mind that I do not want to throw away, thinking they will come in handy later. My psyche is cluttered with thrones and pedestals. This lumber is the reception room for the eucharistic Lord. How must God react? "It should be known," writes St. John of the Cross, "that God dwells secretly in all souls. . . . Yet there is a difference, a great difference, in His dwelling in them. In some He dwells alone, in others He is not alone. Abiding in some He is pleased; in others He is displeased. He lives in some as though in His own house, commanding and ruling everything; in others He is like a stranger in a strange house, where they do not permit Him to give orders or do anything."[5]

---

[5] *The Living Flame of Love*, 4, 14; in *The Collected Works of St. John of the Cross*; 713.

I am uneasy as I reluctantly think about this. Perhaps I owe an apology to Him because He had to come to such a cluttered place. Besides, the Church encourages me in this moment to be like the humble centurion or the repentant prodigal son. So I can ask before the Holy Communion: Lord, only say the word, so that I am healed, sanctified, and freed from the lumber of noisy yearnings and deafening desires silencing the voice of Your love.

POUNDING WAVES

God's love for us is so great that through the Holy Spirit, He transmits it day and night. His love is really special in the Blessed Sacrament. He wants us so much. His love is like gigantic sea waves pounding and demanding to break into our lives. However, we have interior resistant walls resulting in inner conflicts. These conflicts can cause inner pain. These waves want to break down our interior barriers.

I once posed a question to myself about this mysterious eucharistic presence in the Mass continuing in the tabernacle. If He revealed what is truly going on, I would probably get a shock or become rather dizzy. I would see that between my kneeling in the church and the tabernacle there is nothing other than an apparent silence. That is because I have a noisy, possessive preoccupation with and adoration of persons and things. **God's eucharistic love** wants abundantly to be united with me. It is like huge waves **trying to** penetrate and **flow into my life**. He wants to use my weak faith to flow through me with enormous power, to share abundantly this marvellous grace to flush out that noise going on within me. Then I will "see" that Real Presence.

God becomes great for me insofar as I hunger for Him, crying out, "I need You!" Ultimately, the value of this prayer is related to the depth of my faith. This prayer would be different on the lips of St. Francis of Assisi. After all, his thirst for God was so great that he became madly in love with Him. That is what gave meaning to his life. "I need You" on his lips was completely different from a similar prayer on mine. That was because his desire for God was unimaginably deep.

My life reflects the state of my prayer. I need to dispel many illusions. I have to go through many trials of faith, much emptying of being wrapped up in myself so that my prayer gets much deeper. These trials and purifications should help to intensify my desire for God. It is really not surprising that this one whose only desire is that I desire and need Him will work in my life like huge waves striking rocks. They are striking, spraying foam everywhere, flowing in repeatedly just like the ocean shores. One may wonder how it is that these waves never weary, endlessly smashing against the shores. God's love is just like that.

It is really only after my death that I shall see how these enormous waves of God's incomprehensible love for me, overflowing from altar or tabernacle, strike my inner rock to penetrate and flow into my soul. Which is more stunning, this interminably unyielding love of God, unweary like the ocean striking the rocks, or this strange resistance of the rock against which the waves endlessly strike so forcibly?

When I enter church to meet Jesus in the Eucharist, my senses deceive me. What I see and hear tell me nothing about God's action in my life. That is because I do not see these forceful big waves. I do not hear their roar as they strike my rocky surface. I think I am in silence now but that masks the reality. How can God's crazy love for me be idle? How can this incomprehensible love leave me in my veneer of calmness? How can it leave me in my anxiety to be somewhere else?

As I kneel with this idea I am in silence; my eucharistic God tries to crush this noise in my heart. My earthly idols create it by my longings, desires, and fears. If I do not turn away from it, it may force its way into my heart so that although I am in church physically I am mentally far from Him. Anxiety over earthly problems obscures God. Planning important affairs covers Him up completely. God becomes insignificant. I may completely obscure Him in my preoccupation with problems.

Moreover, I am also taken up with faraway thoughts when I think I am so close. I don't realize that I am preoccupied with idols. I think I am craving to focus on prayer. Yet even the words "focus on prayer" hide a snare of the evil one. I can focus on prayer or just on God. "Focus on our own praying." "That is good," the evil one whispers. I should remember that by focusing on my praying I am still far away, searching for idols that cause my distractions. After all, so much thought about my idols and my prayer activity are both ways of being taken up with myself.

I can be physically present in the church but far away in spirit. The obstacle is whatever is taking up my thoughts. God has crazy love for me. I am more or less crazily in love with everything that is not God. Can we resolve the problem?

I visit church and nothing happens. I say it is difficult for me to pray. I think I do not know how to contact God. My prayer is somehow not getting going. I am like a blind and deaf man. Yet God hidden in the Eucharist roars like those huge waves. The roar can be so loud that it deafens my senses. They don't hear the cannon boom on the battlefront. God in the tabernacle under the species of bread roars like the waves: Your belief in me is too shallow. That is why your prayer isn't getting through. You don't really believe I am here, body, blood, and Divinity. You don't believe that decisions are made right here before the altar or tabernacle. You are blind because you eagerly seek human approval. You are ready to kiss doctors' hands to save the life of your mother even though they do not decide what will happen to her. Here, in the tabernacle, you have the one upon whom everything depends—your fate, your mother's, and the fate of these doctors. Yet still you rate the doctors more highly.

So God is still very unimportant for me.

God tells me, Your faith is so tiny it is hardly visible. You are asking like that father in the Gospel: if you can, heal my son (Mk. 9:22). *If you can?* With belief in the Eucharist, nothing is impossible. Yet you do not really believe in my strength and love. So your prayer is not effective. Your prayers don't come from much faith.

St. John of the Cross calls people like me sensual. With my sight I just see the tabernacle doors, nothing more. God is too unimportant for me because I overrate myself. I think I can deal with my problems better than He. Yet He is the one from whom I should seek help. God's huge roar and overflowing waves can destroy my false prayer. My prayer is little more than the movement of my lips with some feelings. I don't have much faith. If only I would admit this. If only I understood what God is trying to tell me in my distractions. He is broadcasting on a different wavelength. He is broadcasting on the gigantic waves of mercy, and where am I?

There is no contact. God bellows with the roar of huge waves as in the Apocalypse: "I will come to you and remove your lampstand from its place, unless you repent." (Rev. 2:5) So to stop believing in myself, I have to cease analyzing my prayer. I am reluctant to admit it. So much analysis focuses on myself and impedes grace. I need to open myself to the striking eucharistic truth that God's loving heart is beating just for me.

When we watch ocean waves, we can feel the fury in them, the powerful upheaval that would like to break something. Yet it is not like that in God. There is simply amazing love for me that is not getting through. Still, perhaps I can manage to accept the grace of faith and then something from that roar will hit my stony heart. Perhaps I shall then start asking forgiveness, I shall humble myself before this astonishing love which like those waves is continuously running towards me from the Eucharist. Maybe there will be a miracle so I will become smaller. Maybe my hard heart will soften. Huge waves will no longer be painfully striking the hardened surface of my heart, but they will gently flood over these crumbling stones from which my heart is now being reshaped. Perhaps they will be really different, more gentle, more humble. The waves won't now strike with force. They will flow over and into me. They will wash me. They will penetrate my inner being. They will shape something unusual from me—something I would never have begun to imagine even in my wildest dreams.

FAITH "TOUCHES" GOD

Even if I have really good insights, my union with God is just on the surface if it is only theoretical. Faith is my need. By faith there is real contact with God and His love.[1]

I may know someone very well, know his history, temperament, likes and dislikes, relations, family, and job. I might even say that I know everything about him. But if, for example, we were climbing a mountain together and I got into difficulties, and the result was that he saved my life, and later I was able to do something big for him, a close bond of friendship would grow. I would begin to realize that I didn't even really know him before these later events. The close bond keeps growing.

---

[1] St. Augustine, *Sermones*, 243, 2: *Tangit Christum, qui credit in Christo*—"He touches Christ who believes in Christ."

Similarly, it is not enough just to know God from books, theology, and deep treatises. These things may make me shine with an outstanding knowledge that remains superficial and theoretical. To find God in depth I need to grow in faith.

To find interior spiritual life, I need faith. Moreover, I need it continually in the beginning and end of my way to God. According to St. Teresa of Avila, achieving sanctity is with the same faith as it was at the beginning, only perfected and deepened. Love is a perfecting of faith. They are always inseparable. That is because both touch the divine.

Through faith I am united with God. I grow more deeply into Him through love, but the foundation and root of my supernatural life, my contact with God, will always remain dependent on faith. One cannot build without foundations. If I try to deepen in love of God without deepening my faith, everything will fall apart.

As I adore the Eucharist, this faith will go on deepening. This may be only the beginning but in deepening this same faith, I find hope and love. I will be seeing God on the altar more and more. Faith in His presence in this sacrament of love will finally reach union with

God, my union of likeness in love.[2] I will participate in God's life as faith increases. That is the sense in which the Eucharist sustains and supports me on the way to sanctity.

It is not enough to be at Mass or adoration. One needs also to deepen the bond with God through acts of faith concerning the Eucharist and adoration. One needs much greater openness, trying to accept the flow of graces He so generously wishes to grant.

From St. Thérèse of Lisieux we may learn about openness to the flow of grace. She depicts Jesus at the top of a flight of stairs with a small child trying to clamber up. The child keeps sliding down. He is doing two things at the same time, trying to climb and trying to fix his eyes on Jesus. This fixing of the eyes is explicitly or implicitly calling out, "I need You." The child continues calling, "I need You," until Jesus comes down the stairs and takes him in His arms. They are united. This descent of the Lord was caused by a child's hunger. They become inseparable.

I make acts of faith yet I cannot imagine my faith deepening. Quite the opposite, I have the feeling that

---

[2] Cf. St. John of the Cross, *The Ascent of Mount Carmel*, II, 5, 3.

the more I try, the more I move backwards. Worse still, I am worrying about it. I even agonize over it. This is my search for God. Finally I lose myself and stop concentrating on whether I am moving towards God or not.

I can make acts of faith at home and as I am contacting people and at work. Yet acts of faith in the presence of the living God are of a quite different order. Deepening faith before God in the Eucharist is really important because then and there I am right at the source and summit. The same God with whom I want to unite is personally present, dazzlingly close. No words can describe it.

God is love, and love is infectious. This is love's characteristic feature. If love ceased to infect, it would cease to exist. I can only find the power of God's love by faith. St. John of the Cross writes that "faith is that admirable means of advancing to God, our goal."[3] There is no other way to union with God. Faith is the only entrance gate to God's love.

I need to look at the altar in a different way. I need to look at it in the light of faith. Dag Hammarskjöld, the

---

[3] *The Ascent of Mount Carmel*, II, 2,1; in *The Collected Works of St. John of the Cross*; 155.

Secretary General of the United Nations, defined faith in an unusual way. Basing it on St. John of the Cross, he said, "faith . . . is God's marriage to the soul."[4] I am to believe that faith is somehow being in love with God. For a bridegroom, the fiancée is the closest, dearest, indeed everything. His focus is only on the girl he is to marry. Meanwhile I don't see God on the altar. My vision is so obscure because I am not in love with Him.

I am looking at the altar and I cannot see anything. My mind is all over the place. I feel nothing because my senses are not enlightened by faith. I have no vision of God. Faith is planted into the mind, but it goes further than the mind. It reaches the first cause, God. It is grafted into the mind, as a branch onto a tree, so it is getting sap from the tree.

Faith is grafted on the mind just like one grafts a vine sprout onto a grapevine. Faith makes the mental vine develop and grow. The stem and roots remain. An incision is made into the plant. A cutting from another vine is grafted in. After a month or two, what was grafted in has grown. If wild shoots come out, they

---

[4] Dag Hammarskjöld, *Markings*, New York: Vintage Books, 2006; 165.

must be cut off, as they weaken the original stem. The vitality comes from the sap spreading from the roots. It gives life to what has been grafted in.

A similar thing happens with faith that is grafted on the mind. The act of faith is more than the intellect. It is a broadened, deepened intelligence. Faith doesn't need to understand. Intelligence is deepened, widened, and empowered by faith.

This power of faith is clear with the woman suffering from a hemorrhage (cf. Mt 9:20–22). Of course, the power of faith doesn't always heal. We don't necessarily receive what we ask for. Yet this power of faith "touches" God like the woman who had a hemorrhage touched Jesus. The contact is real.

Divine contact, says St. John of the Cross, can take place in darkness. This darkness is very like the times when my prayer is dry. I feel nothing. It is like darkness all through me. Many people experience exactly this. There is contact but I do not feel it. This is spiritual darkness. Many say: "I cannot pray since I don't feel anything. I do not pray at all. I am sitting and nothing is happening." Yet if there is a real act of faith, it always somehow "touches" God.

Through faith I "touch" God in a dark sort of way. Somewhere finally, the discovery comes in the form of heavenly happiness. Faith is finding God in darknesses which lead us to the glory of happiness in heaven. Faith is the initiation into and the route to heaven. It is starting right away, here and now, the happiness our eucharistic Jesus longs for me to have.

"Where Do You Live, Teacher?"

Leaving John the Baptist to follow the master, the first disciples were thirsty to hear more. John pointed to Jesus as the long awaited hope of the chosen people. Hope was raised in their hearts: maybe He is the Messiah. With some trepidation they ask, "Teacher, where do you live?" and Jesus invites them: "Come and see." (Jn. 1:38–39)

It is more important for them to meet Him than to discover where He lays His head. They were in the desert. They were leading a very different sort of life from us. This teacher of theirs lives in some sort of tent or shack. We can imagine that He will spend time with the two friends praying in the normal way at that time in Israel—holding the home liturgy in which Jesus sings verses from the Psalms. The two respond to the compelling invitation to become disciples.

Isn't this reminiscent of the meeting with Jesus in the Eucharist? The Liturgy is very simple, and yet its very simplicity gives it something special though unenlightened by faith. It is somehow similar to the simple kind of meeting in the master's abode. The expected one does not reveal glory to them, and there is something similar in the eucharistic celebration as it focuses on the unusual action at eucharistic prayer. The worship of God in word and prayers grows into the greatest act of love. Human action makes way for the divine. "This action of God, which takes place through human speech, is the real 'action' for which all of creation is in expectation."[1]

We are not used to God's enlightenment through faith. The event taking place on the altar appears to be so ordinary. What I see there doesn't lead me to imagine angelic choirs and the accompanying glory. But this is the one who is worthy to receive all glory (cf. Rev. 4:11). I don't see angels, hear them sing, or see their extraordinary adoration. But I have to force my way with prayer, which is a fight of faith towards this invisible reality, imperceptible to my senses. Both signs and symbols which I experience during the eucharistic sacrifice don't

---

[1] Joseph Cardinal Ratzinger, *The Spirit of the Liturgy*, San Francisco: Ignatius Press, 2000, 173.

speak so strongly as to be unveiling the reality that is coming into being. Neither is the word I hear capable of expressing the depths of the reality on the altar.

No wonder then that Pope Benedict XVI praises the value of silence so much.[2] This silence helps in the face of my seemingly helpless words. Words, not able to arouse me in the course of this unusual mystery, can give way to something more effective—silence. Silence can fill me with grace.

It is interesting that Christ's attitude has such strong impact when calling other disciples like Nathanael. To this disciple who asks, "How do you know me?" He replies: "Before Philip called you, when you were under the fig tree, I saw you." (Jn. 1:48) The description of this calling sounds like the announcement of the future glory that will reveal Him: "Because I said to you, I saw you under the fig tree, do you believe? You shall see greater things than these." (Jn. 1:50) You'll see when you are holding the Eucharist after the coming of the Holy Spirit, Nathanael. Then you will be able to see "heaven opened, and the angels of God ascending and descending upon the Son of man." (Jn. 1:51)

---

[2] Ibidem, pp. 211–216.

God tells of His glory and about angels ascending and descending over the Son of man; He tells about Jacob's ladder that leaned against the earth. It is a sort of earthly liturgy reaching up to heaven. Genesis tells us about the experience of Jacob who saw angels ascending and descending the ladder and that Yahweh was in this place (cf. Gn. 28:10–17).

Through much prayer in the school of faith I learn that the Eucharist is where I, like Jacob, could experience the Lord. Yet in reality I don't resemble those two disciples at all as I believe I know where the Teacher-God lives. The miracle of the Lord's closeness has gone stale in my life. Routine has greatly undermined me so that I don't ask as they did. Yet maybe someday I shall be so tormented by everyday life that I will search for Jesus and keep on asking: "Teacher, where do you live?" I will have asked like those whose experience in this first meeting with Jesus led them even to remember the time it occurred. Despite that, the time and place of the meeting were not surrounded by glory. Jesus was present in the poverty of his simple abode. There was no tabernacle. That presence of the God-Man, even when in a great artistic tabernacle, doesn't tell of the reality of His glory in that desert simplicity.

For discovery of the glory of His presence on the altar, I have personally to become very poor. Then I shall see how much the Eucharist influences my life. The Eucharist, the sacrifice, the presence, and the feast should all shed light on my everyday decisions and capabilities. This light will increase the more I am taken up with the spirit of true evangelical poverty. Evangelical poverty is powerlessness. Money, position, abilities, and prediction oppose it. The impact of Eucharist will be making me poorer. The poor who don't know what tomorrow will bring, have no supplies, can't see the future, and are waiting every day for bread—there is no absent-mindedness for them when they ask for daily bread in the Lord's Prayer. In the Lord's Prayer, Jesus tells me to ask to wait for God's bread every day. It will be given to me first of all in the Eucharist.

I will be given poverty as my faith deepens, and I will obtain a certainty. Nonetheless, on the other hand, I will also be full of uncertainty and unable to predict. Evangelical poverty seems to be powerlessness, but only through a human outlook apart from faith. To me it seems that when I can't do anything, I am weak. I feel bad, as it is unpleasant for my self-esteem. Yet if I keep trying to live in evangelical poverty, I may see the hidden power of it, the power that arises through not putting up resistance to grace. That means the Lord is waiting for me in the Blessed Sacrament, seeing that I choose that royal path of poverty which opens the gates of His kingdom. "Blessed are the poor in spirit, for theirs is the kingdom of heaven." (Mt. 5:3)

Maybe I do not even guess that in following the path of evangelical poverty, I am coming closer to the heights offered me in the eucharistic sacrifice and Holy Communion. As it is, the small and poor govern the world since God can't refuse them a thing. They have nothing for themselves, so they can have everything for themselves and everybody else.

It is in this pathway of evangelical poverty that the eucharistic Jesus wants to embrace me. Because I have nothing, He wants to give me everything, not just His gifts but the gift of His very self. This is the one who desires nothing so much as to reign in my spiritual poverty, finally uncluttered. Here and now that will be for me nothing short of a foretaste of heaven. Happy are the poor to whom the kingdom belongs. That is because God abundantly blesses the poor in spirit.

PART IV

THROUGH THE CONTRAST

Despite having been more and more drawn into things of the world, I feel a deep inner yearning to break free. I am frequently, often unconsciously, deeply yearning for something more. I even yearn for sanctity, for God himself. St Paul says it all: "Where sin increased, grace abounded all the more." (Rom. 5:20) Increasing sinful secularization attracts even more of God's mercy and a greater flood of graces. How right St. Augustine was. I am more or less consciously searching for this One without whom my heart finds no peace.[1] Suddenly I find what I have been looking for. It is in Christ's gift of himself in the Eucharist. This is where He can touch me with his love. Such is the activity of grace.

---

[1] St. Augustine of Hippo, *Confessions*, I, 1.

It means that my contact with the Eucharist is as extraordinary as St. Gregory of Nyssa describes it when he notices that finding God consists in ceaseless searching for Him.[2] I will see that the benefit of searching is in the very searching itself. In this way I will understand, as St. Gregory of Nyssa reminds me, that as I step forward I always have the impression I am just starting. My endless yearning actually becomes more desirous the more it is satisfied.

Searching for Jesus throughout my eucharistic life, I have finally found Him in continually searching for Him. It is just like that with the Lord's activity in the Blessed Sacrament. It gives me grace in an apparently unusual way. Later on, some day, I will find its full meaning. For now I find it in searching. He will be hiding himself from me, but at times there will be moments when He reveals himself.

If I am searching for God, I just cannot make do with what I see. I have to push beyond. Forcing my way towards what is really happening on the altar requires quietening this interior noise flowing into me from the world so that the miraculous Eucharist becomes more

---

[2] St. Gregory of Nyssa, *Homiliae In Canticum*, 8 PG 44,941 C.

apparent. Thus by silence I can grow into the grace of faith. The grace flowing from the Eucharist must quieten me so that I see more of the eucharistic gift that opens the gates of heaven before me. Despite all my misery I have great opportunity in the Eucharist to help me to sanctity. Through faith I see another world allowing me to gain access by anticipation into that world of glory.

This is the way for me. I discover what is happening on the altar and then it disappears. I will find in order to search still more. I will begin to discover what priceless grace is heading towards me from the eucharistic altar. Thanks to the power of God, I will be able more clearly to see the liturgy telling about the new coming of the Lord, reminding me that **time is short**. Since the liturgy is about the new coming of the Lord, I will react differently in my moral life. In my everyday life, the Eucharist will give me insight and guide me along the pathway.

Therefore we say: "Lord Jesus, come in glory." These words should show me the senselessness of chasing after earthly life. Eucharistic graces and awareness of the Lord's coming show me a different picture of reality and push me towards the eucharistic vision of the world.

I hope I will finally discover the Eucharist to be the real answer to my longing for sanctity. The longing exists despite any personal feeling of infidelity, selfishness, and sin. The contrast is between the not very admirable self I see and God himself who is the quintessence of purity and love even to the point of loving me in my poverty. Such poor ones He wants to lead through the event of the Eucharist, to the summits, to a deep bond with himself.

A famous violinist once stood before an audience, obviously expecting bursts of adoration for his genius. But what happened surpassed everybody's deepest expectations. In the tension of his performance, the violinist suddenly felt something break under the bow. He felt the instrument wasn't responding. He suddenly realized that one of the four strings had probably broken and this meant that someone must have cut it halfway through. Then came another shock. Another string broke. Someone had cut that one too. Someone wanted his downfall. But he kept playing as if nothing had happened and finished the brilliant performance. No one had even noticed the problem.

When the violinist lifted up the violin showing the two hanging strings, the audience was astonished. There was an eruption of rapturous applause one thought would never end. To play an instrument with such perfection outshone everybody's wildest dreams. Even more, the audience broke all conventions by rushing towards the violinist, unable to believe that such inspiring music could come from a broken instrument. So the maestro's glory was even greater, the weaker the instrument he used.

The law of contrast is that the poorer the human instrument, the greater God's glory. He can create masterpieces from poor human instruments. Isn't it strange that God so much desires that I could serve like this? Not only by surpassing imagination, He wants to surpass every analogy too. He wants nothing less than astonishing communication of the glorious love He so much wants to share.

I am naturally, deeply opposed to this contrast as I don't want to be a poor instrument in God's hands. In God's plans we are to become the basis for revealing the greater glory of this One. This is what I find so hard to believe. I just do not believe that He is leading me in this absolutely incomprehensible way. He does not want this for himself. He only wants this for me. This is the only way I can discover more of His true face. I find it so unimaginable that God is only deeply discoverable in every moment on any of this world's altars in what seems to be nothing less than insane love.

The more fully I adore God, the more I let Him discover within me my likeness to such a violin that no one can play. He is looking for those who are unsuitable for anything, for those unwanted by the world. He is looking for the poorest violinist so that His all embracing glorious love can brilliantly penetrate into our world.

Although I am a violinist who plays poorly, my relationship with the Lord Jesus is also poor though I don't see it. Yet the Lord doesn't reject me. If I can reveal my unbelief, then He himself will say within me, "my Lord and my God." Thus I can make the greatest profession of faith in the whole New Testament.

God never ceases wanting to reach to the depth of human misery. He shows it in the incident of the sinful Samaritan woman. The deeper the abyss, the greater amount of God's loving glory can be transferred. By filling up this human abyss with something humanly incomprehensible, He reveals the enormity of His abundant grace. He wants me to realize the truth about myself. Only that insight can lead me to closer union with Him. God's economy is still looking for poor instruments; the poorer the better. For God, the glory the genius received from the audience playing with two strings is nowhere near sufficient. He wants to play the violin that has no strings at all. Then the brilliant reality of His glorious love becomes apparent. He himself cuts the strings halfway through to play the masterpiece of the divine concert. Then we humans quieten down and silently listen to God. He who is love itself can thus share His embraces within that necessary silence. Thus we begin to discover the extraordinary miracle of the Eucharist.

There are souls who humanly speaking think there is no way out of their traumatic situation. They wallow in a mess of evil and sins of great negligence in their lives. They seem so possessed with evil that there is nothing for them. Jesus awaits them in the Eucharist, turning with special love to bring them to salvation.

And me? I am so **unworthy** so You can save me, Jesus. I am asking You, pleading with You: grant me Yourself in the Eucharist, unite with me by Your grace.

His searching for us is so strange, finding the worst of us in order to make them saints! There is no greater thing than making saints of the most unworthy of us.

Thus He reveals himself in all His glorious abundant love. Nothing is impossible for Him, nothing. So the most unimaginably indifferent or anti-God person, overcoming arrogant resistance, can by grace, if he doesn't put up resistance, become the most magnificent masterpiece of God. That person can become a part of God's unimaginable brilliance on this planet. The greatest glory for God are those who are particularly unworthy and yet allowed to be fully sanctified.

You Give Me Everything

O n the night He was betrayed, He took bread and gave You thanks and praise—he is lowering his voice, he is focusing on the Lord in the Upper Room. Suddenly he is aware of increasingly strange movements and restlessness in the congregation. He tries not to think about it . . . **He broke the bread, gave it to his disciples**—our incomprehensible one is coming to the altar—**and said: TAKE THIS, ALL OF YOU** . . . the walls start to tremble—**AND EAT IT**. He hears someone screaming out, "O my God, what is happening?"

He crouches as if to cling to the altar: **THIS IS MY BODY** . . . the congregation is obviously much disturbed. Something is happening. The wooden double doors creak and crack. **WHICH WILL BE GIVEN UP FOR YOU.** He raises the host. A chunk of plaster falls nearby and covers one side of the altar. With lightning speed he remembers that according to the original Greek Jesus says: **which is being given up for you**. It is being given **now**! He tries to avoid being aware of crumbling walls as he genuflects with increased adoration. He feels glued to the floor. The church empties. He feels the tremor of the altar slab. There is shouting coming from outside. **When supper was ended**— maybe this is the last Mass—**He took the cup**—he is trying to speak slowly, adoring with deepest faith. His unworthy hands are holding God himself. He shows the chalice to an empty church.

Above, there is a raging gale. There is another stronger tremor. Plaster is falling on the altar. He protects the sacred species by covering chalice and host. He doesn't want them to be buried under the rubble. **May this sacrifice**—saying the words, he is transfixed— **advance the peace and salvation of all the world.** The words strike with great force. This is the sacrifice **to the whole world**. What power is flowing from the altar! Now he is alone, alone with God. It is never been like this.

Hear the prayers of the family You have gathered here before You—there is no congregation. His throat painfully contracts. He can't speak. In a moment, the ceiling will collapse and crush him. The left wall of the church is already cracking. Debris covers everything with dust. He has just enough time to cover the host. Painfully, he utters the eucharistic prayer from memory.

"He was not in the earthquake," he told me half a year later. "As with Elijah, God came in a silent breeze. I found scared people huddled together in little groups. I said to them, 'The Lord is with you.' I showed them the corporal and consecrated elements. They gathered around to receive." I have brought you God. He remembers the words. **May this sacrifice . . . advance the peace and salvation of all the world.** What power flows from the eucharistic altar! God has saved you. I have a strange certainty that no one has died.

Everything comes from Him, the earthquake and the Elijah-type silent breeze. He is alive in these small hosts.

I experienced those moments of dread as though it were the end. Perhaps you did, too. But it was only the announcement. At a certain moment when the darkness covered the inside of the collapsing church, I thought it was the end; yet it was also the beginning. I have nothing. Only He is really important. He is importance itself. Everything else is as if finished.

Every Eucharist is the announcement of future life. We should have all died. Yet the sun is still there; the silent breeze is there too. Yet more, He is giving himself to you. Everyone of you is receiving God in your mouth.

It is a great grace to experience such "final" moments. God can extract tremendous spiritual responses from them. The power of experiencing that I am always alone before God, and everything else too, just like you, right now, today, is that He is always recreating and loving me. He loves you and leads you through the narrow pathway He mentions, a pathway which certainly goes forever towards eternal life.

God's light is so strange; a collapsing church, symbol of an ever transient world, the altar hardly scratched. God is present there under the sacred species, the symbol of His endless power and love. Love gushing from the altar.

More than reading books, you will best learn about God by receiving the Eucharist. God comes to you in Holy Communion, accepting you as if speaking: You are receiving everything. Do you need anything else?

I gave them God while their faces were strangely illuminated. I looked back at the rubble and said: Everyone of us takes life for granted. Let's live only for this One who through thick and thin, always creates and loves. You give me everything. God gives himself so that in himself there is the whole world and all creation, recreated.

Everything is given me from You.

You sin because you do not let Him love you.

When I am coming down steep stairs, You are present all the time. You are present in every conversation, in every word that is uttered.

My life is simplified to this: receive Your love whenever I can.

You will never love Him. You are to receive this love in things great and small.

Live just to receive this love.

The Savior's love is the love of the eucharistic Christ.[1] In it you will find happiness and union with Him here and now, on earth.

---

[1] John Paul II used the term *Christ-Eucharist* in the *Address of John Paul II at the meeting with the delegations to the Eucharistic Congress*, Wrocław, June 1, 1997.

The prayer, "Everything I am given comes from You," expresses the meeting of limitless love with your human love. This limitless love is embracing you and your loving response.

You speak to me: "I have only you," which is why You give me everything.

I Have Only You

Everything I am given comes from You. In every moment, You never stop loving me personally. Your love is hard to express. You seem to say, "I am giving you everything as I have only you."

Only You are God. This means that You alone give me everything.

I want to accept it in the silence of my heart. God is the silence, so I will not hurry, as haste shatters the silence and impedes His presence. I have to venerate Him in what He gives me. This only one, I Am, is somehow present in His gift. In taking from Him, I am somehow close to Him.

My ability to write, move my hand or leg, also comes from You. It is thanks to Your love that I am able to get up in the morning. It is You who give me contrition, the grace of forgiveness and pain when I am walking away from You; You give me my willingness to return. You give me the grace to shake off all temptations to sadness and despair. If I am drowning in temptations, I can call out: "You will save me! After all ,You have only me."

When I focus on Him and on what He gives me, it is difficult to sin since only He is in my consciousness. He gives me everything. Without Him and what He gives me, I just couldn't live.

There is only You, God. Of course there is the world, the work of Your wisdom, Your love, where I meet You, where You give me everything abundantly. Apart from this, the world does not exist for me.

I can't live on my own. You give me everything. You want to give me everything. You are the eucharistic mercy.

I can't love You. I know that my "love" is to receive Your love, ever wider, ever deeper.

You give me everything. This consciousness brings me peace, freedom from worries, unrest and fears.

Your love born from the Cross never stops flooding to me from the altar. Yet I seldom take note of it.

You give me everything. You arrange it so that attracted by Your love, I continually open my arms to absorb more of this eucharistic love. It penetrates through and through. Finally I will be completely absorbed and taken over by it.

He gives me everything but gradually He will want to show me there is a hierarchy of gifts. Moreover, there is one miraculous gift that is the source of them all. In opening myself each day to these I shall see something quite different. I shall discover the gift of the redeeming cross, that gift of the Son's sacrifice for me.

I will then discover this reality of God on the altar. Only then will I see the reality of this gift. Then, among the prayers of the Mass I will find where I rest, one to One in eucharistic love. Only then will I understand that divine whisper. It is only for those who live in silence: I have only you. Those gifts were the gifts of daily life as I never cease loving you, but here, I have become the gift for you.

Amazed By This Love

I am really shaken when I begin to realize that in the palm of my hand is He, the one true God who rules the micro- and macro-world, the One upon whom every nerve and tissue depends. Finally I may get to see that He allows me to adore Him in the palm of my hands at least for a moment as He only has me. He only has me. I am everything for Him. I need Him to be everything for me. He comes to me in an unexpectedly riveting way. I try to respond to these unusual words of His love. After all, I have nothing, nobody; truly I have only Him. If I lost Him, I would not be able to live.

Once I discover the reality of eucharistic presence; once I discover that this is the same love with which He loves me and only me, I will see that the Eucharist doesn't cease to be the gift for the mystical body of

Christ. Once I discover the amazing love of Jesus present in the Eucharist I will discover that the Eucharist doesn't cease to be homage of adoration. In this adoration you can find a little corner, where He whispers: For you I died, just for you. Everybody says dying for everybody is like dying for none. Yet I have only you. I, the God who reveals to you my incomprehensible love in the Eucharist, am really present. I, the world's ruler, am master of heaven and earth. Still, I find you to be priceless. I take care of the whole world yet I tell you, I have only you.

Maybe I will believe it because various events like human ways are by no means smooth and straight. Yet these events, marked as they are with extraordinary victories of grace and my stubborn lack of cooperation, nonetheless keep telling me that He is ceaselessly burning with love for me. At last I can get enraptured by this eucharistic love. I will see it is humanly speaking quite insane for Him to fall in love with the likes of me. Yet this love expresses itself in transfixing words. This infinity of God ruling from the eucharistic altar throughout the world, directing the smallest element of macro- and micro-history, and in this context, this constant whisper of His: I have only you.

It is not possible finally to fail to fall in love with this sacramental, eucharistic, incomprehensibility. Worlds come and go, yet eucharistic love goes on forever. Above all, it is all just for me. This crazy gift is forever revealed in these words: I have only you, **I have only you**.

ABOUT PARACLETE PRESS

WHO WE ARE

PARACLETE PRESS is a publisher of books, recordings, and DVDs on Christian spirituality. Our publishing represents a full expression of Christian belief and practice—from Catholic to Evangelical, from Protestant to Orthodox.

We are the publishing arm of the Community of Jesus, an ecumenical monastic community in the Benedictine tradition. As such, we are uniquely positioned in the marketplace without connection to a large corporation and with informal relationships to many branches and denominations of faith.

WHAT WE ARE DOING

BOOKS | Paraclete publishes books that show the richness and depth of what it means to be Christian. Although Benedictine spirituality is at the heart of all that we do, we publish books that reflect the Christian experience across many cultures, time periods, and houses of worship. We publish books that nourish the vibrant life of the church and its people—books about spiritual practice, formation, history, ideas, and customs.

We have several different series, including the best-selling Living Library, Paraclete Essentials, and Paraclete Giants series of classic texts in contemporary English; A Voice from the Monastery—men and women monastics writing about living a spiritual life today; award-winning literary faith fiction and poetry; and the Active Prayer Series that brings creativity and liveliness to any life of prayer.

RECORDINGS | From Gregorian chant to contemporary American choral works, our music recordings celebrate sacred choral music through the centuries. Paraclete distributes the recordings of the internationally acclaimed choir Gloriæ Dei Cantores, praised for their "rapt and fathomless spiritual intensity" by *American Record Guide*, and the Gloriæ Dei Cantores Schola, which specializes in the study and performance of Gregorian chant. Paraclete is also the exclusive North American distributor of the recordings of the Monastic Choir of St. Peter's Abbey in Solesmes, France, long considered to be a leading authority on Gregorian chant.

DVDS | Our DVDs offer spiritual help, healing, and biblical guidance for life issues: grief and loss, marriage, forgiveness, anger management, facing death, and spiritual formation.

Learn more about us at our Web site:
www.paracletepress.com, or call us toll-free at 1-800-451-5006

You may also be interested in . . .

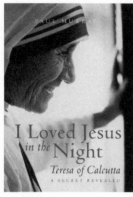

I Loved Jesus in the Night
Teresa of Calcutta,
A Secret Revealed

By Fr. Paul Murray

ISBN: 978-1-55725-579-2
$18.95, Hardcover

I Loved Jesus in the Night is one priest's compelling account of meeting with the saint of Calcutta. Sharing anecdotes and first-hand experiences, Paul Murray offers a glimpse into why Mother Teresa could declare, in one of her letters, that if ever she were to "become a saint," she would surely be one of "darkness."

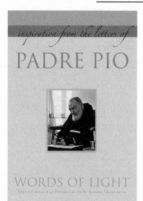

Words of Light
Inspiration from the
Letters of Padre Pio

Compiled and with an Introduction
by Fr. Raniero Cantalamessa

ISBN: 978-1-55725-643-0
$14.99, Paperback

The world was startled in 2007 by revelations that Mother Teresa of Calcutta's spiritual life was full of serious doubts and personal suffering for nearly 50 years. The other great saint of the last half century—Padre Pio—offers similar revelations of his own in this enlightening collection of short excerpts from his letters.

Available from Paraclete Press
www.paracletepress.com | 1-800-451-5006